PENGUIN BOOKS

Mots d'Heures: Gousses, Rames

Born in Mexico City, Luis d'Antin van Rooten was raised in the United States, where he lived in New York City and Chatham, Massachusetts. Along with his obvious interest in the scholarship of language, Mr. van Rooten pursued a distinguished career in the theater and movies. He appeared in many Broadway plays, and his movie credits include *City Across the River*, *The Sea Chase*, and *The Night Has a Thousand Eyes*.

François Charles Fernand d'Antin

MOTS D'HEURES: GOUSSES, RAMES

The d'Antin Manuscript

DISCOVERED, EDITED, AND ANNOTATED BY

Luis d'Antin van Rooten

PENGUIN BOOKS

Penguin Books Ltd, Harmondsworth,
Middlesex, England
Penguin Books, 40 West 23rd Street,
New York, New York 10010, U.S.A.
Penguin Books Australia Ltd, Ringwood,
Victoria, Australia
Penguin Books Canada Limited, 2801 John Street,
Markham, Ontario, Canada L3R 1B4
Penguin Books (N.Z.) Ltd, 182–190 Wairau Road,
Auckland 10, New Zealand

First published in the United States of America by
Grossman Publishers 1967
Published in Penguin Books 1980
Reprinted 1980, 1981, 1983, 1984

LIBRARY OF CONGRESS CATALOGING IN PUBLICATION DATA
Van Rooten, Luis d'Antin.
Mots d'heures, gousses, rames.
French verses constructed to reproduce phonetically
a selection of Mother Goose rhymes in English.
Bibliography.
Includes index.
1. Macaronic literature.   2.   Nonsense-verses.
3.   Nursery rhymes—Anecdotes, facetiae, satire, etc.
4.   Parodies.   I.   Mother Goose.   II.   Title.
[PN1489.Z7V36   1980]   398'.8   80-19273
ISBN 0 14 00.5730 7

Printed in the United States of America by
The Murray Printing Company, Westford, Massachusetts
Set in Janson

For

C.　G.　K.　V.　R.
L.　G.　V.　R.　E.
　C.　K.　V.　R.

Affectionately.

◄[*Foreword*]►

To detail the exact manner by which "The d'Antin Mss. Mots d'Heures:[1] Gousses, Rames"[2] came to my hand would be too tedious and of but little moment here. Suffice it to say these curious verses were part of the meagre possessions of one François Charles Fernand d'Antin, retired school teacher, who died at the age of ninety-three in January of the Year of our Lord, 1950, while marking papers.[3] Some three years later, as the only surviving relative of the deceased, I received his personal effects through the kind offices of Maître Théophile Gustave Pol Plôn, Notaire, of Aix-en-Provence, Bouches-du-Rhône, France.

The pitiful little packet remitted to me included a ribbon-tied bundle of love letters from one Luisa Contempré, soprano, who died of tuberculosis while "en tournée" in Athens, Greece; a holograph of Napoleon III; some postcards marked "Vues de Naples et de Pompéi"; and a prescription for falling hair. All these I consigned to the eternal discretion of my fireplace. An excellent recipe for turbot in saffron found welcome in my kitchen archives, and the thin sheaf of fragmentary poems here presented soon became the object of intriguing study and speculation.

[1] "Words of the Hours." A more poetic title than the more familiar "Book of Hours." A religious or philosophic background is tacitly indicated by this title.

[2] "Gousses, Rames." A "gousse" is a clove or section, as in the bulb of the garlic plant. We can therefore assume that this implies "Root and Branch," or a complete unity. Alas, would only that the poems had come down to us so.

[3] The vestigial remnant of an occupation, become the escape mechanism of an academician's senility.

What are they? Who wrote them? When? These are but a few of the many questions they evoke.

The "Mots d'Heures" are written in an antique and scholarly script on a few sheets of handmade paper, Canson et Montgolfier, watermarked 1788. If they are earlier in origin (a decided Gothic flavor makes this an almost imperative assumption), the transcriber of these fragments has so modernized the words as to make it impossible to date the verses on the basis of orthography. The cryptic phrasing, the disconnected thoughts, the mysterious allusions to places and people suggest at first an affinity to the prophetic quatrains of Nostradamus. On the other hand, violent epigrams were a popular form of insult in those centuries when wit was sharp but life was cheap. Again, they may be the salty, mundane commentaries of some earthy prelate, who nonetheless dreaded the "auto-da-fé," should his ideas be circulated too freely. Finally—they may be the creations of some Gothic cultural link midway between François Rabelais on the one hand and James Joyce on the other.

The most fascinating quality of these verses is found upon reading them aloud in the sonorous, measured classic style made famous by the Comédie Française at the turn of the century and whose greatest exponents were Coquelin, Lucien Guitry, Mounet-Sully and the divine Sarah; these poems then assume a strangely familiar, almost nostalgic, homely quality.

I present the "Mots d'Heures," therefore, to the public, as fully annotated as careful research permits. Although my work on them has reached a dead end, I sincerely hope some more perceptive scholar, with the help of my notes, will bring greater clarification to these esoteric fragments. *"Che altro con meglio pletro cantara."*[1]

For their encouragement, assistance and inspirational criti-

[1] Dante. *The Divine Comedy.*

cism, I wish to thank my good friends, Romney Brent, actor and linguist; Frederick Posses, attorney-at-law; various and Sundry members of the American Federation of Television and Radio Artists (AFL–CIO); and Miss Beauty Love Johnson, laundress.

L. d'A. V. R.

Cabot Hill
Chatham, Mass., 1966

Un petit d'un petit[1]
S'étonne aux Halles[2]
Un petit d'un petit
Ah! degrés te fallent[3]
Indolent qui ne sort cesse[4]
Indolent qui ne se mène[5]
Qu'importe un petit d'un petit
Tout Gai de Reguennes.[6]

---

[1] The inevitable result of a child marriage.

[2] The subject of this epigrammatic poem is obviously from the provinces, since a native Parisian would take this famous old market for granted.

[3] Since this personage bears no titles, we are led to believe that the poet writes of one of those unfortunate idiot-children that in olden days existed as a living skeleton in their family's closet. I am inclined to believe, however, that this is a fine piece of misdirection and that the poet is actually writing of some famous political prisoner, or the illegitimate offspring of some noble house. The Man in the Iron Mask, perhaps?

[4,5] Another misdirection. Obviously it was not laziness that prevented this person's going out and taking himself places.

[6] He was obviously prevented from fulfilling his destiny, since he is compared to Gai de Reguennes. This was a young squire (to one of his uncles, a Gaillard of Normandy) who died at the tender age of twelve of a surfeit of Saracen arrows before the walls of Acre in 1191.

Eau la quille ne colle
Oise à mer est haulte de soles
Aîné marié au sol, vas-y![1]
École vorace paille
Pain école vorace boule
En école vorace fille de loterie.[2]

Et vérifie d'allure, ah! des fidèles
En avarie faille ne fille te l'a dit
Et puis, tu lui dis, tu lui dis, vingt-deux filles de loure.[3]
Oh! d'hère, se nom soeur erre
Ascain compère
Huit qui ne collent et ne se fient de loterie.[4]

---

[1] An eldest son, wedded to the family estates by primogeniture, is here urged to seek adventure. The general area in which he lives is clearly identified by the Oise River, a tributary of the Seine, navigable for most of its length. A truly poetic image is created by the first line and the promise of a sea teeming with Channel sole in the second line.

[2] Here he is warned of fish that will rise to any lure, but also of voracious schools of lottery girls. Evidently, he is to seek adventure *and* a wife.

[3] He is told to study their bearing, so many having failed or come to grief, who might have been faithful. He is particularly warned

against twenty-two dancing girls, perhaps some notorious corps de ballet of the period.

⁴ The country boy is told not to give his name to an erring sister. The good example of his pal from Ascain (small Basque town in the foothills of the Pyrenees, not far from St.-Jean-de-Luz) is set before him. He didn't get stuck because he didn't trust to luck.

Eh! dites-le, dites-le,

De quatre et méfie de le.[1]

Haine de caoutchouc[2] me Douvres[3] de mou.

Le lit le dos que l'a fait de[4]

Tous s'y sèchent à c'port[5]

Et de digérant,[6] ohé! Ouida,[7] ce pou.

In this fragment our poet reveals himself as an incurable Anglophobe. Note well the many inferences:

[1] Four as a mystic number has had, in the superstitious lore of many countries, a sinister or unlucky quality. I point out two instances in literature to bear out this premise. "The Sign of the Four," Arthur Conan Doyle, 1889. And the interesting fact that Dumas titled his novel about Athos, Porthos, Aramis and d'Artagnan, "The *Three* Musketeers." Sheer superstition. In this case, however, it is obvious that the reader is warned against the four major divisions of Britain, i.e., England, Ireland, Scotland, Wales.

[2] Guttaperchaphobia. A morbid dislike for cleaning fish. (Rich. Holland, Univ. of Chi., 1945.) A barbed comment on British culinary practices.

[3] A seaport, 76 miles E.S.E. of London, famed as one of the Cinque-Ports, pop. 39,950 (1938). This, the usual port of entry from France, is also noted for its soft chalk-white cliffs.

[4] They've made their bed, let them lie in it!

[5] This may be a reference to the dry, phlegmatic character in the traditional concept of the English "milord," or a comment on the notorious roughness of a Channel passage.

[6] On the other hand, this may be a play on words—and the port of the kind used by the British as a digestive, imported at Dover.

[7] Ouida is the pen name of Louise de la Ramée, 1839–1908, English novelist. Both her pseudonym and patronymic indicate French origin, and it must be one of her male antecedents (because of the gender) that our poet calls a louse. Probably for migrating to England.

Oh, les mots d'heureux bardes
Où en toutes heures que partent.[1]
Tous guetteurs pour dock à Beaune.[2]
Besoin gigot d'air.
De que paroisse paire.[3]
Et ne pour dock, pet-de-nonne.[4]

---

[1] Minstrels were no doubt a happy lot, and it is not surprising that France, a cradle of wit and culture, could turn them out in such numbers that they came and went on an almost predictable schedule. As one came in the portcullis, another left by the oubliette.

[2] Beaune. Town in the Côte-d'Or, 11,000 pop., famed for its wines and mustard. It is not a port, therefore, why should everyone watch its docks? Certainly it does not have any particular renown as a center of contraband.

[3] This must refer to the Côte-d'Or, a peerless parish indeed. Rich in some of the finest vintages of France and, if we are to believe the previous line, a great lambing country.

[4] Pet-de-nonne. An extremely light and fluffy pastry. Although any decent French housewife would ask for them without hesitation at her favorite pâtisserie, delicacy forbids a direct translation here.

Des rois élus dolmen,[1] Hunyadi lit d'élégant[2]
À Nice boue lette se remède fauve laide, laide, laide.[3]
Y vin tout de brou[4] qu'est nid chaud et lit de doux que[5]
Rat trou demi de lave de aide, aide, aide.[6]

Écart y dit homme, Tour Iseult où aillent feux jaunes
En bas doré phare fort tout Mecque, Mecque, Mecque.[7]
Doux rose de lit de doux qui a de chouriner brou que
Et nid de goton fâcheur de direct, direct, direct.[8]

[1] To the elected kings a dolmen. This is one of the very few times that these ancient stone monuments are given a regal rather than religious significance. Between the two, the truth probably lies.

[2] The elegant bed of the Hunyady. A Hungarian family of great historic distinction; its most famous member, John Corvin (1387–1456), led a crusade against the Turks and defended Belgrade. His son Matthew became King of Hungary. They certainly could afford decent furniture.

[3] Nice needs no introduction. It is one of the world's most famous seaside plaisances. The poet, moreover, claims great therapeutic values for its mud.

[4] A liquor made by steeping the outer rind of walnuts and held in great esteem by medicinal herbalists.

[5] Another reference to a bed or nest—could this be addressed to a professional invalid?

[6] A rat hole through lava helps. To get to the Nicean mud?

[7] Setting it aside, the said man goes to the Tower of Isolde where yellow fires burn at the base of a golden lighthouse, much like all Mecca.

[8] Still another reference to soft beds and the cutting up of walnut hulls, and then the mention of a vagabond's bed that angers by its directness ends this curious rhyme.

Despite the effective device of repeating the rhyme words, the context is so confused that there seems to be no cogent explanation for this piece of mystifying versification.

Et qui rit des curés d'Oc?[1]
De Meuse raines,[2] houp! de cloques.[3]
De quelles loques ce turque coin.[4]
Et ne d'ânes ni rennes,
Écuries des curés d'Oc.[5]

[1] Oc (or Languedoc), ancient region of France, with its capital at Toulouse. Its monks and curates were, it seems, a singularly humble and holy group. This little poem is a graceful tribute to their virtues.

[2] Meuse, or Maas, River, 560 miles long, traversing France, Belgium, and the Netherlands; Raines, old French word for frogs (from the L., *ranae*). Here is a beautiful example of Gothic imagery: He who laughs at the curés of Oc will have frogs leap at him from the Meuse river and

[3] infect him with a scrofulous disease! This is particularly interesting when we consider the widespread superstition in America that frogs and toads cause warts.

[4] "Turkish corners" were introduced into Western Europe by returning Crusaders, among other luxuries and refinements of Oriental living. Our good monks made a concession to the fashion, but N.B. their Turkish corner was made of rags! This affectation of interior decorating had a widespread revival in the U.S.A. at the turn of the century. Ah, the Tsar's bazaars' bizarre beaux-arts.

[5] So strict were the monks that they didn't even indulge themselves in their arduous travels. No fancy mules nor reindeer in *their* stables. They just rode around on their plain French asses.

Jacques s'apprête
Coulis de nos fêtes.¹
Et soif que dites nos lignes.²
Et ne sauve bédouine tempo³ y aussi,
Telle y que de plat terre, cligne.⁴

---

¹ *Coulis,* a sort of strained broth. Jacques was either a sauce chef or an invalid.

² Jacques was also an alcoholic, since his thirst is beyond description.

³ He was fond of Arab music.

⁴ He believed the earth was flat. The last word of the line, meaning "wink," is obviously a stage direction. Poor Jacques, whoever he was, was obviously considered a fool.

Pis-terre, pis-terre
Pomme qui n'y terre[1]
Ah! de ouilles[2] fenil[3] coup ne qu'y perd[4]
Il peut terrine et pomme qu'y n'échelle[5]
Iéna équipe soeur verrou elle.[6]

---

[1] Woe to the earth left to lie fallow. It is not quite clear whether a lack of apples or potatoes is meant.

[2] *Ouiller* (verb). The practice of filling a half empty wine barrel with wine of the same vintage up to capacity. Air tends to sour wine.

[3] *Fenil.* A hay press or baler.

[4] Nothing must be wasted?

[5] *Terrine* refers, of course, to the earthenware cooking pots of French farm kitchens, and apples that need no ladders are, we suppose, windfalls. These must be gathered and made into conserves.

[6] Iéna, town in Thuringia, Germany, pop., 70,000. Famous for its manufacture of optical and precision instruments. Also Napoleon I's victory against the Prussians in 1806. In the balance of the line, "to equip a sister with a bolt (or latch)," the poet refers to the use of chastity belts, in this case of German silver. In bold, broad strokes we have here a magnificent portrait of the thrifty, cautious French farmer.

Terre, vasée, Krous qu'est dément[1]

      En y vaquer Krous qu'est d'émail.[2]

Il fondu Krous qu'est de si que se pince,[3]

      Agacer Krous qu'est déesse taille[4]

Il botté Krous qu'est de quatre.[5]

      Vich côté Krous qu'est de mousse[6]

Année olive tous guetteurs[7]

      Déracinés Krous qu'est délit Toulouse.[8]

---

[1] Krous, or Kroumens, natives of the Ivory Coast, were highly prized as slaves, because they were good workers and excellent navigators. This fragment is a saga of slavery, a Krous is driven mad by being taken from his native swamp.

[2] He is described as having a skin like enamel.

[3] He is melted by another Krous who is pinchable, and

[4] who is built like a goddess.

[5] His interest must have been returned, for now he has to provide two pairs of shoes.

[6] They end up near Vich, a small town in Catalonia, Spain.

[7] For a whole year they watch over the olive trees.

[8] Here the writer accuses a native of Toulouse, ancient capital of Languedoc, with the crime of uprooting these poor natives.

Lit-elle messe, moffette,[1]
Satan ne te fête,
Et digne somme coeurs et nouez.
À longue qu'aime est-ce pailles d'Eure.
Et ne Satan bise ailleurs
Et ne fredonne messe. Moffette, ah, ouais![2]

---

[1] *Moffette.* Noxious exhalations formed in underground galleries or mines.

[2] This little fragment is a moral precept addressed to a young girl. She is advised to go to mass even under the most adverse conditions in order to confound Satan and keep her heart pure until the knot (marriage) is tied. She is warned against long engagements and to stay out of hayfields, be they as lush and lovely as those of the Eure valley, for Satan will not be off spoiling crops elsewhere. She must not mumble at mass, or the consequences will make the noxious fumes of earth seem trivial.

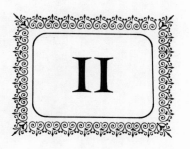

II

Chacun Gille[1]

Houer ne taupe de hile[2]

Tôt-fait, j'appelle au boiteur[3]

Chaque fêle dans un broc,[4] est-ce crosne?[5]

Un Gille qu'aime tant berline à fêtard.[6]

---

[1] Gille is a stock character in medieval plays, usually a fool or country bumpkin.

[2] While hoeing he uncovers a mole and part of a seed.

[3] Quickly finished, I call to the limping man that

[4] every pitcher has a crack in it. If a philosophy or moral is intended, it is very obscure.

[5] "Is it a Chinese cabbage?" It is to be assumed that he refers to the seed he found.

[6] At any rate he loves a life of pleasure and a carriage.

Amboise élite gueule, chic à d'élite écoeure-le
Ratine d'émis de l'eau va fort raide.
Oing chinoise goutte, chinoise béribéri goutte
Beau douane chinoise batte, j'y vais aux rides.[1]

[1] The poet reveals his feelings quite clearly anent the élite. He finds their elegance disgusting and their red clothing with a high nap stiff and uncomfortable. Their taste for Oriental ointments, fancied exotic maladies and childish attempts to smuggle their purchases makes him grow old before his time. The high moral tone of these fragments precludes the assumption that it might be just envy.
Compare Horace's "*Persicos odi, puer, apparatus . . .*"

L'île déjà accornée . . .[1]
Satinées cornées . . .[2]
Y dîner guérisse masse bâille . . .[3]
Il se taquine costumes[4]
Et ne poule d'août des plumes[5]
Et ne ses doigts des gouttes beaux émaille.[6]

[1] The (lord of the) island already has horns. This would seem to be a rehash of the old Tristram and Iseult legend; however, it is so fragmentary that positive identification is impossible.

[2] "Satiny corneas" for "velvet eyes," obviously a partial description of the lady in the case.

[3] Yawns help digest a heavy dinner: a thumbnail sketch of the dull, lethargic husband.

[4] He was teased about his clothes. He was not only dull, but sloppy and inelegant.

[5] He looked like a moulting chicken in August.

[6] She wore nail polish! An interesting revelation of the antiquity of cosmetics. The Egyptians used enamel-like paints; the Chinese, jeweled guards. The timeless universality of nail decoration, alas, gives us no clue as to the possible date of these verses.

Raïa[1] qu'écorce turban béret crosse[2]
Toussez afin laide y appeau[3] nez ouate torse.[4]
Rhinanthes heure fine guerre,[5] sans bel sonneur tôt.[6]
Chiches.[7] Lave moujik où est révère chicot.[8]

[1] Name given to non-Mohammedan Turks.

[2] We must assume that this fragment describes a Turkish convert who forsook the turban for the biretta and crozier of a bishop and whose greatest fame was as a missionary.

[3] *Appeau.* A whistle used as a bird lure. Although his voice was ugly and he suffered from a bad cough, he must have achieved some fame as a preacher.

[4] This would indicate a singularly homely man with a stuffed nose as big as his body. Poetic license permits a certain amount of exaggeration, after all.

[5] *Rhinanthes.* A common European weed, sometimes called a "cock's-comb." This is a very obscure phrase and must refer to some incident during or just after a war. Perhaps this weed overran a battlefield somewhat like the poppies of Flanders after World War I.

[6] There is no doubt that this refers to some primitive mission church which had no bells.

[7] *Chiches.* Chick-peas, the staple item of diet among primitive peoples and missionary monks, known in Europe from earliest historical times.

[8] This man apparently converted and baptized an obscure Russian tribe given to worshipping tree stumps. A curious survival of Druidic religion.

Tine, queue,
T'est Laure.[1]
Salle de jeu,
C'est l'or.[2]
Riz chemin
Pour mène
Bec à romaine
Dive.[3]

---

[1] "Tail of a vat thou are Laura." Last one in at the wine pressing?

[2] "In a gaming room it's gold that counts."

[3] A rice road (a trade route is indicated) leads a Roman nose to the divine. Since large noses have been considered, from the most ancient times, to symbolize acquisitiveness, the reference to gambling becomes clear. This is possibly an incantation to the gods of chance.

Reine, reine, gueux éveille.
Gomme à gaine, en horreur, taie.[1]

---

[1] "Queen, Queen, arouse the rabble
  Who use their girdles, horrors, as pillow slips."

Pas de caïque, pas de caïque,[1] bécasse,[2] mâne,[3]
Bec ami est coquille[4] à ce vaste Assise ou Cannes[5]
Roulette[6] et n'épate[7] éden[8] marcou[9] y débit.[10]
Aîné petit inédit, oh, vaine![11] fort bébé ennemi.[12]

---

[1] *Caïque*. A long narrow boat commonly used in the Levant.

[2] A shore bird, the snipe.

[3] *Mâne*. In Roman mythology, the soul after death, i.e., a ghost.

[4] "The beak is friendly to shells." Birds have been the subject of many poems, and here tribute is paid to a ghostly snipe which does its own wading and swimming and feeds on shellfish.

[5] Its range is from Cannes on the Riviera to Assisi in Italy, shrine of St. Francis, patron of birds.

[6] A gambling game made famous by the Casinos of Monte Carlo and the Riviera.

[7,8] Comment that such an attraction (roulette) is unnecessary in this astonishing earthly paradise.

[9] This refers to a man with a magic symbol on his body who is believed to have supernatural powers, but note that

[10] even he suffers losses.

[11] From the eldest to the yet unborn—All is Vanity.

[12] I don't know what child psychologists would have to say on this subject, but this bears out a suspicion I have long harbored. Babies hate people! It would be interesting to know at what age this hatred turns to dependence and affection, or whether it persists in the subconscious, subject to reawakening by the pressures and tensions of our age.

Mise treize mairie quoi y êtes contrée riz[1]
Ah! d'azur garde en gros[2]
Huit Silvère belles en écho[3] que l'échelle
Un preux, Diomède, Alain héros.[4]

[1] Undoubtedly this refers to a very heavy rice tax, payable at the town hall.

[2] *Azur* here must refer to the heraldic arms of the town which kept most of this rice crop. Such tax burdens were not unusual.

[3] Silvère (saint), pope in 536 A.D., died of hunger in 537 A.D., feast day June 20. Here eight beautiful natives of the province are identified with this famous saint, probably because of similar deaths.

[4] The lord of the province is compared to Diomedes, ancient king of Thrace, noted for his cruelty, whom Hercules fed to his own horses. In this particular instance, the situation was saved by a courageous knight named Alain, who used a ladder to scale the castle walls. A simple story of oppression and rescue.

Raseuse arrête, valet de Tsar bat loups
Joues gare et suite, un sot voyou.[1]

---

[1] This is a description of an incident at the Russian Imperial court. A valet beats off some wolves, while the lady barber is asked to stop shaving the Tsar. The last three words chide the stupid oaf of a valet for interrupting so delicate an operation (haemophilia was a scourge of the Imperial family). The wolves were really at fault, but this was only one of countless occasions when men were unjustly persecuted, making the revolution of 1917 inevitable.

III

Tam-tam, de paille personne
Est-ce tôle, épigone, et ouais! y runes.[1]
D'épi que noisette, en état moabite.[2]
Et ne témoins d'Ukraine dom de strict.[3]

---

[1] These two lines can only be interpreted if we use the colloquial or slang meanings of two words. (a) *Tam-tam*, actually a Chinese gong, also signifies a scandal! (b) *Tôle*, usually sheet metal, is commonly used in argot as a term for prison. The lines now read: Scandal! The straw man, a son (*épigone*), went to jail for unrevealed reasons. Runes, in the ancient Goth sense of the word, meant "hidden things."

[2] This refers to the use of wheat grains and nuts in divination in the Near East. Divination was a common practice in early trials.

[3] Simply, the witnesses were brought in from outside the country, and the judge (in this case a churchman) was severe. We can come to only one conclusion: secular justice, tempered by prejudice and superstition, was corrupt.

Myriades évitent lames
Et nuisent feux lisses.[1] Où asseoit et sonne haut.[2]
En abreuvoir dettes mairie ointe
Deux lames azures d'Iago.[3]

[1] That thousands avoided the sword and spoiled smooth fires is an obvious reference to the Inquisition.

[2] Here choir stalls are indicated, if the inference above is accepted.

[3] To satisfy debts (spiritual?), the mayoralty anoints two blue steel blades of Iago. Without a doubt, Santiago, patron of Spain, is meant. The exact relationship of the Inquisition to the civil courts has long been a matter of conjecture and study. In this case exoneration by a civil authority not only indicates close association between the secular and lay justices, but also hints that the defendant was a powerful and important personage.

Grosse apache,
Drôle de lâche.[1]
Six bas de foire onze épines
Thé qu'occupe
Trinquez dupe.[2]
D'encolure née beurre usine.[3]

---

[1] The reference here is probably to the Parisian criminal and not to the American Indian. The savagery of both is proverbial.

[2] Cases in which stockings were used as weapons by stranglers are cited by many eminent criminologists. Thorns are used in various ways as a means of torture in crimes of extortion, and the tea in which a dupe is toasted is, in this context, nothing but a Michel Finn.

[3] The mention of shoulders or neck relates back to the implied strangulations above, but the citing of "butter factory" cannot be clarified; at least not without a *granum salis.*

Si sot, mare, je ris d'eau
J'hoquet, chat lave ennui mât stère.[1]
Et châle Ève bêta panne y aider
Bécots.[2] Si Carnot turc et n'y fasse taire.[3]

---

[1] This curious little item starts out as a drunkard's song, laughing at water, and hiccupping, while the family cat washes itself out of sheer boredom on the wood pile. *Stère* is a wood measure (1 cu. m.), similar to our cord.

[2] His stupid woman with her shawl is in an awful mess because she kisses promiscuously! Probably the psychological reason for his alcoholism (or vice versa).

[3] This is a very cryptic phrase, unless we tie together two very far-fetched analogies. Nicole Carnot, French mathematician, was the first to postulate the principles of thermodynamics. The water cure is attributed by our poet to the Turks. And it is this application of a plethora of water that will silence our songster.

De cuit neuve Ar / / chimède sommes Tarse
Allons, et submerge idées.[1]
De neuf veuf Ar / / istote de Tarse
Hindou qu'incline aux haies.[2]
De qui n'oeuvre Ar / / cole fort de Tarse.
Un bête de naïf fut l'essor
De nef avor / / té brouette bagues de Tarse[3]
En va haut de style nos morts.[4]

---

[1] While drunk, Archimedes studied some Arabic formulas from Tarsus (birthplace of St. Paul) and submerged some ideas, thus discovering the principle of specific gravity. Since most of our arithmetic was developed in Asia Minor, this is not at all impossible.

[2] "When newly-widowed Aristotle heard from Tarsus of a Hindu who bowed to hedges." Aristotle's famous comment, "the more I find myself by myself and alone, the more I have become a lover of myth" is thus completely clarified.

[3] The builder of the fort at Arcola (scene of one of the victories of Napoleon's Italian campaign) was from Tarsus. Hired to build a church, his was the springline of an abortive nave; he used a barrowful of cheap Asia Minor jewelry. No doubt he was trying to take advantage of a method proposed for the building of the Duomo in Florence. The church was to be filled with dirt and the dome built over the resulting mound. Small coins were to be scattered through this earthen core. When the dome was completed, the poor of Florence would cart the earth away for the sake of whatever money they could find (see: *Vasari's Lives*. Brunelleschi).

⁴ The eternal attempt to escape the "*Memento, homo, quia pulvis es et in pulverem reverteris.*"

Note. This is the only verse in which the caesura is used, although it is a fairly common convention in classical poetry.

Oh, Anne, doux
But. Cueilles ma chou.[1]
Trille fort,
Chatte dort.[2]
Faveux Sikhs,
Pie coupe Styx.[3]
Sève nette,
Les dèmes se traitent.[4]
N'a ne d'haine,
Écoute, fée daine.[5]
Éléphant tue elfes
Dit qu'en Delft.[6]
Tartines, fortunes,
Miséricorde d'une.[7]
Fit vetîmes Sixtine
Médecine quitte Chine.[8]
C'est Fantine est d'Inn
Mais Arouet dîne.[9]
Nanini, Toine est dit,
Met plâtres, sème petit.[10]

We can only consider this series of proverbs and epigrams in rhymed couplet form as a garland or bouquet of versified wit and wisdom.

[1] A tender dedication to the poet's muse.

[2] An early version of "When the cat's away, etc., etc."

[3] "Mangy Indians, Pius cuts the Styx." An attempt to impress unbelievers with the powers of the Popes over pagan mythology and superstition.

[4] This could be assumed to mean, "When the sap rises, the people (*demos*, Gr.) rejoice."

[5] "Harbor no hate, good fairy." In this instance, she appears as a doe. It was the common practice of fairies and sprites to assume animal shapes.

[6] "Only in Delft is it believed elephants kill elves."

[7] "Bread or money, give charity of one or the other."

[8] "We caused the Sistine to be dressed (i.e., decorated). Medicine comes from China." This unquestionably refers to Sixtus IV, saint and pope, 1414–1484. Just what influence he had on the pharmacology of his time is hard to determine. It is known, however, that the Chinese at that period were far more advanced in medicine than their European contemporaries.

[9] Fantine must have been a great beauty from the Inn River valley in central Europe. In any case, Voltaire preferred to continue dining. He must have been a very old man at this time.

[10] Nanini (Giovanni Maria), c. 1545–1607, Italian composer and for a time choirmaster of the Sistine Chapel. It would seem that Italians have always been called Tony, and it was automatically assumed that they liked to work in plaster and were generally improvident, since they sowed little.

D'Arras en halte, oh humaine, où Liévin échoue![1]
Chiale semaine[2] . . . y Gilles de Rennes chez Diderot[3] . . .
    ouate tout doux.[4]
Chiffrer de sombre eau[5] . . . Ouïe d'Aoudh[6] . . . Denys
    brette[7]
Si huppe bémol sans délit[8] . . . Enceinte aime tout bête.[9]

---

[1] Arras and Liévin are important towns in the Department of Pas-de-Calais. Is this a prophecy of some sort?

[2] "They wept for a week." It is not clear whether the natives of Liévin are intended or whether it refers to

[3] Gilles de Rennes, obscure member of an ancient and noble family—at one time the Dukes of Britanny. Diderot, encyclopaedist and philosopher. No reason is given for these two men to visit or know each other. We must assume either that the nobleman sought knowledge or that Diderot sought a titled patron. The latter seems improbable, if we consider that the seeds of the French Revolution germinated in the writings of 18th century French intellectuals.

[4] Cotton is soft.

[5] "To calculate dark waters" can only mean to navigate unknown seas.

[6] Aoudh. One of the ancient divisions of India. The natives are not particularly noted for their keen hearing.

[7] The sword of Denys. Unquestionably St. Denys, apostle of the Gauls, first bishop of Paris, III cent. A.D.

[8] *Huppe* is a tuft, as on a bird's head. *Bémol*, of course, is a flat in music. I call this to the attention of naturalists. If, in a mutation

from mating-calls to more showy plumage, male birds become tone deaf, could this not explain the otherwise mysterious extinction of certain species?

[9] At last a grain of sense in this most confusing and obscure of all the poems. "A pregnant woman has strange cravings."

Lait déborde, lait déborde,

Volaille au royaume

Jurassent seize envoyeurs

En dieux! argile d'arène a la gonne.[1]

À l'Aix cèpes tuent ânes[2]

En tasse hisse l'italienne

Hachis et ces crêpes tendres

Douaire mienne qu'à peine.[3]

---

[1] The Roman flavor of this fragment is inescapable. Milk overflows and poultry is shipped in for a great feast following a gladiatorial combat, in which the noble host soiled his long robe.

[2] "At Aix mushrooms killed donkeys." Here a sinister note creeps in, as will be seen in the lines that follow. We are dealing with a case of poisoning, but the people involved were so highly placed that the whole thing is merely hinted at. Not even the exact Aix is identified. Aix (from L., *Acquae*) was used as a prefix for any Roman town where springs of any sort existed. Therefore this incident could have occurred anywhere from Aix-en-Provence to Aix-les-Bains to Aix-La-Chapelle (Aachen).

[3] The Italian woman raised a cup, ate hash and tender pancakes, say lines 6 and 7 quite clearly. Line 8, however, is very ambiguous because of the lack of punctuation and the falacies of translation. It could be:

> "My widow's dower had pain"
> or
> "My widow, her dower? Hardly."

Here lack of punctuation, like the omission of vowels in written Semitic languages, presents an insuperable problem for the translator. Our only assumptions must be based on context—in this example, most vague.

Mander ce châle et ce fer aux fesses
Douze dix châle est-ce folie Grèce
Ouest ne céder ce châle est ce fol huhau!
Tiers dès ce châle a ce farde dégout
Ferraille dès ce châle est-ce l'eau vigne en gui vigne
Sept heures d'est ce châle lueur garde forêt les vignes
Andes châle date est-ce abornant deux sabotiers
Et ce bonnet, en balade, un goût en guais.[1]

---

[1] This little poem is an ode to shawls, their qualities and virtues; they should wear like iron and be long enough to cover the hips. A shawl costing only 12/10 is sheer Greek folly and should be avoided by Occidentals. They should be kept clean and not be smudged with make-up. If shot with metal (threads), the design should be a grapevine or mistletoe, and it will glow even at dusk. The reference to the Andes must, of course, be because of the varied forms of shawls worn by the indigenes—i.e., rebosos, tilmas, serapes, ruanas and ponchos. The last line refers to bonnets, worn on a promenade, as being in the taste of an impotent or sterile herring.

Loup si l'eau quête,[1]
L'ossuaire peau quitte,[2]
Qui dix fissures fendîtes.[3]
D'ardoise, notre peine, ni nitre[4]
Bateau ribaud rendîtes.[5]

---

[1] "If a wolf seeks water." This verse is obviously a collection of evil omens, in this case portending drought.

[2] "In the ossuaries the dry skin falls off the bones." A vivid but macabre word picture indeed.

[3] Ten cracks in the earth. If there are but five, there may be hope.

[4] Here the sorrows of earth are compared to slate, which is petrified mud and nitre or saltpeter. This latter, as its name implies, is a salt that exudes from rocks.

[5] A *ribaud* was originally a camp follower. Today it means anyone who lives a loose, unconventional life. This line can probably be most adequately transcribed as "Rats abandon a sinking ship."

IV

Coeur-lilas, Coeur-lilas,[1] huile d'habit maille.[2]

D'échalotes[3] vache douchesse,[4] nos diètes filles te soignent.[5]

Beauce est en accouchant en soie avoine cime,[6]

Et fit des ponts,[7] c'est trop, Berry,[8] choucas[9] en crime.

---

[1] When knighthood was in flower, they chose strange devices for their blazons. If a lilac heart seems somewhat extreme, I refer my readers to the arms of a certain Herbe de la Pensée.

[2] "Oil up your armor." Sound advice.

[3] Probably a corruption of Astolat.

[4] This Don Quixote de la Mancha saw his Dulcinea del Toboso as she really was!

[5] It was the custom for young maidens to minister unto errant knights, whatever that means.

[6] Beauce (cap. Chartres) was the land of this knight's birth. Although not particularly noted for its silk industry, it is the finest grain-raising region of France, hence the reference to oats.

[7] Ever since the days of Horatio, to defend a bridge was a most desirable exploit in which to display one's dexterity and bravery.

[8] One of the de Berry family was too much for him. Since this was a royal house, it may have been a fatal case of *noblesse oblige*.

[9] *Choucas*. A variety of blackbirds. Probably a blazon in which they appeared neither rampant nor couchant, but *in flagrante delicto*.

Hérissent[1] de cherche, en hérisse de ce type poule,
Aux peines de dehors ennuis rares de pie poule,
Hérisse de personne[2] canapé de stère
En dire haïssent saignisse prêt hier.[3]

---

[1] *Hérisser*, v.t. (L., *ericius*). To stand on end, such as hair.

[2] This is descriptive of a person seized by fear. The skin is like a chicken's (goose pimples?). He is not like a magpie, which in its native state is fearless.

[3] He cowers on a sofa of fair dimension, hating the idea of the bleeding that should have been performed the day before. The fear of pain is a well-recognized human trait, as is the tendency to avoid doctors until it is too late.

S'i' m'plut, ça y m'âne
Mettez paille, m'âne.[1]
Gouaille tout défaire.[2]
Cette s'i' m'plut ça y m'âne
Tout de paille, m'âne.
(Lai, demi-tessiture, ou air.)[3]
C'est de paille, m'âne
Tout s'i' m'plut ça y m'âne.
Lait demi à vieux bénis.[4]
Cède s'i' m'plut, ça y m'âne
Tout de paille, m'âne.
Sérail aveux nos dénis.[5]

---

[1] There can be no doubt, because of the repetitious rhythmic refrain, with its reference to straw and a donkey, that this is a drover's song. Note that the refrain is broken up by simple aphorisms, a familiar device in folk music.

[2] Literally, "Ridicule destroys anything."

[3] By some inadvertence, a comment has replaced the original saying here. It describes the song as a lay or air, in a limited vocal range.

[4] "Blessed by the aged," who can only drink skim milk.

[5] "We are pledged to avoid the Mussulman's palaces." In other words, "It's a rough road to Christianity."

"Adieu, notes laïques," dit d'acteur frêle[1]

D'horizon Hawaii canot tel

Baux, dix anneaux en tonneau. Filou elle,[2]

"Adieu, notes laïques," dit d'acteur frêle.

---

[1] This first line, repeated at the end of the quatrain, can easily be interpreted as saying: "Actors, being frail, bid farewell to convention."

[2] One so hated civilization he fled to the South Seas, like Gauguin and Robert Louis Stevenson. The canoe or raft used is carefully detailed. The last two words of line 3 in literal translation say
"She was a tramp."
But whether they refer to a ship or to the fact that he left town because of an actress, is anybody's guess.

"Pousse y gâte, pousse y gâte,
  Et Arabe, yeux bine?"[1]
"A ben, tout l'on donne
  Toluca de couenne."[2]
"Pousse y gâte, pousse y gâte,
  Oh, a dit Dieu d'hère?"[3]
"Y fraternelle Lydie, Moïse,
  Honneur de chair."[4]

---

[1] Although the dialogue form of versifying is very ancient and quite common, this is one of the few fragments so written. In the first speech, an Arab is chided for planting a crop, then allowing it to spoil, while merely eyeing his hoe. The Arabs are a traditionally nomadic people, not given to agriculture.

[2] In his reply, our hero admits he was building castles in Spain, dreaming of a pigskin from Toluca (famous market town, capital of the State of Mexico, Mexico). These pigskins make excellent water bags—an item of great interest to a desert-dweller.

[3] "What sayeth the poor man's God?" *Hère*, in medieval times, a serf, bound to the lord of a manor.

[4] "There will be brotherhood in Lydia, Moses, blood is thicker than water." Lydia, Middle East region bordering on the Aegean Sea.

Lille[1] beau pipe
Ocelot serre chypre
En douzaine aux verres tuf indemne
Livre de melons un dé huile qu'aux mômes
Eau à guigne d'air telle baie indemne.[2]

---

[1] Lille is one of the great industrial cities of France and must be assumed to be the residence of the subject of this little poem.

[2] We are dealing with a chemist or alchemist, since this can't be anything but a recipe for an ointment or perfume of doubtful magical qualities. The scent sac of an ocelot which produces a disturbingly penetrating odor is squeezed with a quantity of chypre (which ditto) in a dozen containers of flawless volcanic glass. To this is added a pound of melons, a thimbleful of oil (½ oz.), a sweet cherry and the fragrance of unspoiled berries, any kind will do. The verse, unfortunately, gives no clue as to its application. We must, of course, suspect an aphrodisiac.

Papa, blague chipe
À vieux inouï houle[1]
Y est-ce art? Y est-ce art? Trépas que se foulent[2]
Aune format masure, en nouant format thème[3]
En nouant fleur-de-lis de bois de solive en délienne.[4]

[1] Stealing, even in fun, my father, can disturb a mature man to un-heard-of depths. Note how *houle*, the swell and stir of the sea, is used in a highly poetic simile.

[2] "Where is art?" We are dealing with total destruction.

[3] Huts are built of alders or wattles, tightly forming the theme.

[4] Knotted fleur-de-lis carved in old beams after the manner of Delos. As Shakespeare said, "So may the outward shows of earth be least themselves, the world is still deceived with ornament."

Here the poet cries anathema to cheap builders and cheating contractors.

Polis poutre catalane
Polis poutre catalane
Polis poutre catalane
En la sève ti.[1]
Sou quitté qu'étoffe à gain
Sou quitté qu'étoffe à gain
Sou quitté qu'étoffe à gain
Des vols gagne où est.[2]

---

[1] The repetition of the first line to form a quatrain would indicate that this was a song or perhaps a children's game chant. The first verse advises the use of Ti sap to polish a Catalan beam. The Ti plant is common to the South Seas but heretofore has had no virtue attributed to it other than its decorative value.

[2] "A penny taken is the stuff of profit
   There is gain in stealing."
A far cry from "A penny saved is a penny earned." If the first four lines are considered a derision of painstaking labor carried to exotic lengths, the second four clearly make this a thieves' refrain.

Coque: loque de déride or
Loque de déride or.[1]
Haine: chic le chaque logis
À avant-côtes de qui.[2]

---

[1] A hull or shell for the rags of one who spurns gold. Ascetics chose strange dwellings, so that these two lines could refer to a hermitage. The Hermitage also was the name of a Russian Imperial palace.

[2] Hatred toward the sumptuous or elegant home, in front of the unknown foreshore. If we assume beach or sand we get in French, *L'arène*, which is a pun on *La Reine*. Therefore, we can interpret this quatrain as an attack on a Tsarina. Which one, alas, we wish we knew, as it would help in dating these rhymes.

Dissolu typique,[1] Ouen ou Marquette.[2]

Dissolu typique, c'tiède homme.[3]

Dissolu typique a des roses vives.[4]

Dissolu typique, aie de nom,

Dissolu typique, craille

Oui, oui, oui,

À louer: heaume.[5]

---

[1] A typical wastrel, in short, a regular bum.

[2] Ouen (saint), bishop of Rouen, circa 609–683 A.D.; Père Marquette (1637–1675), French Jesuit, discovered the Mississippi. Two moral and saintly men of action to be emulated.

[3] A tepid man. What a matchless description!

[4] Fresh roses are used as hedonist symbols in this context.

[5] The last and, if the pun is forgiven, crowning shame. The craven wastrel, fallen upon evil days, croaks "Yes, yes, yes, my crest is for rent!" i.e., he is willing to sell his birthright—the family jewels having long since disappeared. This verse patently belongs to the age of moralists and essayists, and forms an interesting parallel to Hogarth's famed *Rake's Progress*.

Noyé, l'ami, dans tout, sa lippe,
Après d'alarmants sauts, l'équipe.
En duvet deuil beffroi évêque . . .
Apprête alors ma salle de teck.[1]

---

[1] Here we have perhaps the clearest word picture presented in the manuscript. A simple translation is without doubt the best way to present it. One might almost give it the title, *Lament:*

> "Scornful of life, the friend was drowned
> After alarming leaps by the clique.
> In downy mourning the bishop's tower . . .
> Prepare then my room of teak."

A room of teak is obviously a coffin. The first line, however, could mean that, unlike Shelley, our nameless friend did not drown, but drank himself to death—a much more common and unromantic end.

⊰[*Bibliography*]⊱

Encyclopaedia Britannica, 1952.

Nouveau Petit Larousse Illustré. Librairie Larousse, Paris, 1953.

Webster's New International Dictionary of the English Language. Second Edition, Unabridged, 1949.

Any old Mother Goose.

⊰ *Index of First Lines* ⊱

TIENS, DE

A selection of books published by Penguin is listed on the following pages.

For a complete list of books available from Penguin in the United States, write to Dept. DG, Penguin Books, 299 Murray Hill Parkway, East Rutherford, New Jersey 07073.

For a complete list of books available from Penguin in Canada, write to Penguin Books Canada Limited, 2801 John Street, Markham, Ontario L3R 1B4.

Sheilah M. Hillman and Robert S. Hillman, M.D.
TRAVELING HEALTHY
A Complete Guide to Medical Services in 23 Countries

For the smart traveler who considers health-care needs as carefully as itinerary, this book is the best health insurance available for travel in Mexico, Western Europe, Yugoslavia, Japan, and the Soviet Union. The seasoned traveler, the businessman, the exchange student, or the family on holiday will find here invaluable information on staying healthy: how to prepare a personalized medical kit, manage a chronic illness, find help for a variety of medical problems, fill a prescription, arrange for emergency first aid, and ask for help in fourteen languages. Also included is a list of two hundred commonly used American drugs and their equivalents in all twenty-three countries, plus an illustrated guide to first aid.

Susan Kelz Sperling
Foreword by Willard R. Espy
Illustrated by George Moran
POPLOLLIES AND BELLIBONES
A Celebration of Lost Words

A rollicking entertainment for word lovers, this beautifully designed volume will intrigue everyone who relished the best-selling *An Exaltation of Larks* (also available from Penguin Books). An enthusiastic verbal archaeologist, Susan Kelz Sperling has unearthed hundreds of long-buried treasures of the English language. For instance, *hum* (a strong liquor), if drunk in too large quantities, may cause one's head to *quop*. As *Publishers Weekly* said, "If a reader *glops* one entry, he is sure to *keak* for more. Zestful illustrations by George Moran further tickle the funny bone."

Patrick Hughes and George Brecht
VICIOUS CIRCLES AND INFINITIES
An Anthology of Paradoxes

If, like Oscar Wilde, you can resist everything except temptation, then this book is irresistible, for there is nothing like a paradox to torment and tantalize the mind, to tease the eye, and generally to tie you into knots. Ranging from ancient to modern, the anthology includes aphorisms, such as Groucho Marx's famous remark that he would refuse to join any club that would have him as a member, and traditional logical paradoxes discussed by philosophers from Zeno to Bertrand Russell. "The paradox is an attractive beast, and here is a whole volume of contradictory truths to delight the eye and ear"—*Psychology Today*.

William I. Kaufman
THE WHOLE-WORLD WINE CATALOG

Wine labels contain, says William I. Kaufman, much more information than most people suspect—information that wine-shoppers could put to good use and profit if only they understood the meanings of the words and the symbols. In this easy reference guide to the world of wines, wine labels, and tastings, Kaufman shows us how to interpret the labels on hundreds of wines ranging from Amontillado to Tokay, from vineyards in countries as diverse as Algeria, Argentina, Denmark, France, the United States, Japan, and South Africa. Using this remarkable book, you can be sure of getting exactly the wine you want, within any price range!

Also:

THE TRAVELER'S GUIDE TO THE VINEYARDS OF NORTH AMERICA